Sheila Bewley

The Garden Flower Almanac

LOCHAR PUBLISHING · MOFFAT · SCOTLAND

Published by Lochar Publishing Ltd, MOFFAT, SCOTLAND, DG10 9ED.

A catalogue record for this book is available from the British Library

ISBN 0-948403-81-0

Typeset in 9pt on 10pt Bembo
by Blackpool Typesetting Services Ltd, Blackpool
and printed by Cambus Litho Ltd, East Kilbride

Illustrations by Sheila Bewley

Contents

Introduction

The range of garden flowers available ready grown, as well as in seedling form, from garden centres and nurseries, is enormous. It is now possible for the lazy or inexperienced gardener to fill the garden with instant colour without previously having raised plants from seed or propagated them by other methods. Plant propagation is however fascinating and not necessarily difficult. Most gardeners will want to raise their own plants at some time; notes on the subject are included in this book.

In the interests of keeping the list of plants to a manageable size, flowering trees and the larger shrubs have been omitted, despite the temptation to include them for the beauty and brilliance of their flowers. I have similarly avoided subjects such as bromeliads, cacti and plants that are generally only grown in greenhouses; although it needs to be recognised that certain of the plants featured, such as amaryllis and mesembryanthemum, would not fare well out of doors far north of Devon.

The almanac offers basic information on a wide range of plants. It is intended to be useful as a general guide. The plants are arranged in alphabetical order according to their common names. (Plants which do not have common names or in fact have several are listed under their botanical ones.) Each entry illustrates one plant, with its common name followed by its full botanical name, a general description of the plant and notes concerning its cultivation, propagation and flowering period, as well as an appropriate gardening tip. The basic vocabulary of gardening is defined in the glossary of terms.

In making my selection I have benefited from the wise advice of Kenneth Ashburner (B.Sc [Hort]), as well as from kindly neighbouring gardeners, but the final choice is of necessity a very personal one. My daughter, Emma, gave invaluable help preparing the original typescript.

Agapanthus

Agapanthus   **Liliaceae**

Clump-forming, tuberous perennials with erect
stems carrying large umbels of flowers. Semi-
hardy, some are evergreen in mild areas. Flowers
are usually blue and can be bell, tubular or
trumpet-shaped; leaves are strap-like. For
sheltered beds and borders; also look well in
containers.

Flowering Period: Summer to late summer.
Cultivation: Plant four inches deep, more in
                      cold areas, in moist but well-
                      drained soil in full sun.
Propagation: By division in spring, or raise
                      from seed in spring or autumn.
Gardening tip: Protect crowns in winter with
                      ash or mulch.
Illustration: *Agapanthus orientalis.*

Amaryllis

Hippeastrum   Amaryllidaceae

Genus of bulbs grown mainly for their huge
funnel-shaped flowers although there are some
smaller species. Frost-hardy to frost-tender.
Often grown indoors but can be grown out of
doors in mild areas. Colours ruby to orange-red;
some varieties white with petals striped or tipped
with red or pink.

Flowering Period:	Generally winter and spring; some smaller species in summer.
Cultivation:	Large flowered hybrids should be planted in autumn in well-drained soil in a sunny or partially-shaded site, half burying the bulb.
Propagation:	By seed in spring, or by offsets in spring (summer flowering species) or autumn (large flowering hybrid).
Gardening tip:	When leaves die away, dry off bulb until following autumn. Smaller species should be kept dry in winter while they are dormant.
Illustration:	*Hippeastrum x hybrida.*

Anemone
(Japanese Anemone)

Anemone   **Ranunculaceae**

Fully hardy tuberous or rhizomatous perennials.
The flowers are mainly cup-shaped, sometimes
starry, often with a ring of leaves below. Colours
range from white through red to blue and purple.
Basal leaves are round to oval and deeply cut.
Japanese Anemone *(Anemone x hybrida)* is tall,
vigorous and branching with slightly-cupped
white flowers carried on wiry stems above deeply
divided, dark green leaves.

Flowering Period:	Spring, summer and autumn.
Cultivation:	In moist but well-drained, humus-rich soil in sun or partial shade.
Propagation:	By seed in late summer, division in spring or root cuttings in winter.
Gardening tip:	Very good plants for borders and beds where they can be mingled with lower-growing plants.
Illustration:	*Anemone x hybrida* (Japanese Anemone, flowering late spring/early autumn).

Anemone

Anemone pavonina Ranunculaceae

Genus description as for "Anemone" on previous page. *Anemone pavonina*, featured here, has rather poppy-like dark centred flowers, single or semi-double, in colours that are rich and jewel-like – deep reds, magentas, purples and blues, as well as the paler shades of these colours and white – rising above divided, frilly leaves.

Flowering Period: Early spring.
Cultivation: In moist but well-drained, humus-rich soil in sun or partial shade.
Propagation: By seed in late summer, division in spring or root cuttings in winter.
Gardening tip: Excellent for borders and for cutting.
Illustration: *Anemone pavonina.*

Arum lily

Zantedeschia   Araceae

Tuberous perennials, evergreen in mild areas,
frost-hardy to frost-tender. A dramatic and
ornamental plant often associated with water
gardens, where its glossy, arrow-shaped leaves
make a perfect foil for large, funnel-shaped
spathes surrounding short spadices. A good plant
for containers as well as for planting out.

Flowering Period: Early to mid-summer.
Cultivation: In well-drained soil in sun or
partial shade. *Z. aethiopica* can
also be grown in shallow
water as a water margin plant.
Propagation: By offsets in winter.
Gardening tip: In all but the mildest areas
needs to be brought indoors
over winter; best grown in
large pots for this purpose.
Illustration: *Zantedeschia aethiopica*
(Arum lily).

Aster

Aster   Compositae

Ultra hardy, even invasive, clump-forming
perennials with daisy-like flower heads. Mostly
herbaceous but the genus includes deciduous and
evergreen sub-shrubs. Flowers are in all shades of
pink, mauve, blue and purple. Leaves generally
mid- to dark-green, small and lance-shaped.

Flowering Period: Summer to autumn.
Cultivation: In any fertile soil, moist and
                       well-drained, in the sun.
Propagation: By seed or softwood cuttings
                       in spring or by division in
                       spring or autumn.
Gardening tip: Tall species require staking,
                       and most species must be
                       divided regularly. Popular for
                       borders and as cut flowers.
Illustration: *Aster novae-angliae.*

Astilbe

Astilbe   **Saxifrageae**

Very hardy, clump-forming perennials grown for their fluffy heads of minute flowers, in shades of white, pink and red, which remain handsome even when dried brown in winter. Leaves are compound and deeply cut, bronzed when young, rich green when mature. Decorative seedheads can be left for winter.

Flowering Period: Summer.
Cultivation: In rich, moist (in some cases even boggy) soil in sun or partial shade.
Propagation: By seed in autumn or division in spring or autumn.
Gardening tip: Leave undisturbed if possible, but divide every few years. Mulch annually in spring with well-rotted compost.
Illustration: *Astilbe* "Venus".

Aubrieta

Aubrieta   Crucifereae

Very hardy evergreen trailing and mound-forming perennials popular for rock gardens, banks and walls. A profusion of small flowers, lavender-blue to purple and deep red, is carried on short stems above a mound of small, soft green leaves.

Flowering Period: Spring.
Cultivation: Thrives in the sun in well-drained soil.
Propagation: By greenwood cuttings in summer or semi-ripe cuttings in late summer or autumn.
Gardening tip: Dead-head and cut back hard after flowering to promote compact shape.
Illustration: *Aubrieta.*

Autumn crocus

Colchicum   **Liliaceae**

Fully hardy corms with profuse and showy
crocus-like flowers growing direct from the
ground without leaves (the stemless, strap-shaped
or elliptic leaves appear in early spring and die
down in summer). The flowers are generally
white to purple, sometimes chequered; there is
one known yellow variety.

Flowering Period: Despite the name "Autumn
crocus", colchicums are not all
autumn flowering. Some
species flower in spring.

Cultivation: In well-drained soil in an open
and sunny situation.

Propagation: By seed or division in autumn.

Gardening tip: Best in shrubberies and wild
gardens, as leaves of most
species are untidy.

Illustration: *Colchicum autumnale*
(Autumn crocus).

Begonia

Begonia   **Begoniaceae**

Large, versatile genus of plants grown variously
for their colourful flowers and ornamental leaves,
which are asymmetrical at base. Begonias are
officially classified into the following groups:
(1) Cane-stemmed; (2) Rex and rhizomatous;
(3) Semperflorens; (4) Shrub-like; (5) Tuberous;
(6) Winter flowering. Each group has its own
cultivation requirements. The following notes
refer to SEMPERFLORENS, a very popular
bedding plant; evergreen, bushy perennials, they
are often grown as half hardy annuals. Flowers
are single or double in various shades of pink,
borne upon soft, succulent branched stems with
generally rounded green, bronze or variegated
leaves.

Flowering Period:	All summer.
Cultivation:	In well-drained but moist light soil in sun or partial shade.
Propagation:	By seed or stem cuttings in spring.
Gardening tip:	Pinch out growing tips to encourage bushy growth.
Illustration:	*Begonia semperflorens* (Wax begonia).

Bleeding heart

Dicentra   **Papaveraceae**

Fully hardy perennial, with graceful sprays of
pendant flowers on slender, arching stems. Leaves
are ferny and finely divided. Flowers are in
shades of white and pink or pinkish-red and
white.

Flowering Period:	Late spring and summer.
Cultivation:	Does best in moist, peaty, well-drained soil in semi-shade.
Propagation:	By division when dormant in late winter or by seed in autumn.
Gardening tip:	*Dicentra* reaches thirty inches in height, so is best in a border behind smaller plants.
Illustration:	*Dicentra spectabilis* (Bleeding heart).

Bugle

Ajuga   Labiatae

Fully hardy annual and perennials, vigorous and in some instances invasive. Evergreen or semi-evergreen, forms a creeping carpet of ground cover. Two-lipped flowers are usually blue or, rarely, pink or white, with oblong to spoon-shaped bronze-purple or deep green leaves, sometimes marked with cream and pink.

Flowering Period: Spring.
Cultivation: Will grow almost anywhere, in sun or shade in any soil.
Propagation: By division in spring.
Gardening tip: Can be invasive, so keep growth in check. Purple form of common bugle (*A. reptans*) often used as ground cover.
Illustration: *Ajuga reptans.*

Busy Lizzie

Impatiens   **Balsaminaceae**

Fast-growing, evergreen bushy perennials grown as annuals. Half hardy, with succulent but brittle stems, fresh green oval leaves and spurred flowers in shades of red, pink, purple and white.

Flowering Period: Spring through to autumn.

Cultivation: In moist but not waterlogged soil in sun or semi-shade. Himalayan balsam (*Impatiens glandulifera*) thrives in moist conditions.

Propagation: By seed or by stem cuttings in spring or summer.

Gardening tip: A versatile plant that is popular for bedding and containers and can also be grown indoors.

Illustration: *Impatiens* (Busy Lizzie).

Calceolaria

Calceolaria   Scrophulariaceae

Annuals, biennials and evergreen perennials, sub-
shrubs and climbers, some of which are grown as
annuals. Fully hardy to frost-tender. Most have
rounded or oval hairy leaves, but a few species
have wrinkled, glossy, dark green leaves. All bear
characteristic pouched flowers, generally yellow,
speckled with crimson or brown.

Flowering Period: Spring to summer.
Cultivation: Most like the sun, but a few
                       prefer a cool, shady site, in
                       well-drained soil.
Propagation: By seed in autumn or by
                       softwood cuttings in late
                       spring or summer.
Gardening tip: Incorporate sharp sand and
                       compost into soil for best
                       results. Protect in harsh
                       winters or place in alpine
                       house. Good for sheltered rock
                       gardens.
Illustration: *Calceolaria* (Slipper flower).

Californian poppy

Eschscholzia   Papaveraceae

Hardy annual with filigree glaucous leaves and profuse, cup-shaped flowers in all shades of yellow, orange and pink, popular for rock gardens. Self seeding and invasive.

Flowering Period: All summer.
Cultivation: In full sun in poor, well-drained soil.
Propagation: By seed in spring or early autumn.
Gardening tip: Dead-head regularly to ensure long flowering period.
Illustration: *Eschscholzia papaveraceae* (Californian poppy).

Campion

Silene also *Lychnis*   Caryophyllaceae

Fully to half hardy annuals and perennials grown
for their mass of five-petalled flowers in shades
of pink, magenta, scarlet and white, usually with
a distinctive calyx. Leaves are often in basal
rosettes. Many are mat or mound-forming and
suitable for rock gardens, taller species and
varieties, such as the scarlet *Lychnis chalcedonica*,
for borders.

Flowering Period:	Late summer to early autumn.
Cultivation:	In well-drained, fertile soil in full sun.
Propagation:	By seed in spring or early autumn, or by softwood cuttings in spring.
Gardening tip:	Some species grow particularly well in gardens by the sea, especially *Silene vulgaris*, subspecies maritima.
Illustration:	*Lychnis. Arkwrightii.*

Canterbury bell

Campanula Campanulaceae

Annuals, biennials and perennials, some of which are evergreen, fully to half hardy. Erect, bushy plants with bell-like flowers in shades of blue, pink, mauve and white. Campanulas can be clump-forming, trailing, spreading or mound-forming, making them suitable for a variety of sites, in borders, rock gardens and containers.

Flowering Period:	Spring and summer.
Cultivation:	Most forms like moist but well-drained soil, in sun or shade.
Propagation:	By seed or division in spring or autumn, or by softwood or basal cuttings in summer.
Gardening tip:	Tall varieties benefit from staking. Delicate flower colours are best preserved in the shade.
Illustration:	*Campanula medium* (Canterbury bell).

Carnation

Dianthus Caryophyllaceae

Evergreen or semi-evergreen annuals, biennials or perennials, fully to half hardy, grown for their flowers and in many cases their distinctive fragrance. They comprise two groups: Border and Perpetual-flowering carnations. All are frost-hardy except for the perpetual-flowering carnation. Leaves, which sometimes coil outwards, are narrow, lance-shaped and silvery- to grey-green. Each stem bears several semi-double to double frilled flowers in shades of red, purple, white or yellow. Flowers are classed as selfs, bicolours (with contrasting eye), fancies (with contrasting flecks or stripes), picotees (with petals outlined in a darker colour) and laced varieties (each petal edged with contrasting "lacing"). Good for borders and very popular as cut flowers. The biennial *Dianthus barbatus* (Sweet William) is a relative.

Flowering Period:	Mid-summer (border carnations). All year (perpetual-flowering plants grown in a greenhouse).
Cultivation:	In well-drained, not too fertile soil in full sun.
Propagation:	By seed in spring or summer, or very easily by cuttings of non-flowering shoots, or layering, in summer.
Gardening tip:	Tall forms need staking. Grow well in coastal gardens. When growing for cut flowers, disbud so that there is only one flower on each stem.
Illustration:	Border carnation.

Cerastium

Cerastium   Caryophyllaceae

Fully hardy, vigorous annuals and perennials,
with star-shaped flowers and prostrate stems
covered with tiny grey leaves.

Flowering Period: Late spring and summer.
Cultivation: Must have sun and well-
                     drained soil.
Propagation: By division in spring.
Gardening tip: Grown mainly in rock gardens
                     and for ground covering.
Illustration: *Cerastium tomentosum*
                     (Snow-in-summer).

Christmas rose

Helleborus   Ranunculaceae

Generally ultra-hardy, mostly evergreen
perennials grown for their winter and spring
flowers. Very good in woodlands and wild
gardens. The large, generally lance-shaped
toothed leaflets make good ground cover.
Flowers are cup-shaped with prominent stamens
and thick sepals in unusual and sombre colours –
yellow-green and purple as well as white.

Flowering Period:	Winter to early spring.
Cultivation:	In moisture-retentive soil in semi-shade.
Propagation:	By seed or division in autumn or very early spring.
Gardening tip:	Most deciduous species retain their old leaves over winter, which should be cut off in early spring as flower buds develop.
Illustration:	*Helleborus niger* (Christmas rose).

Chrysanthemum

Chrysanthemum   Compositae

Annuals, perennials and evergreen sub-shrubs
grown for garden decoration, exhibition and as
long-lasting cut flowers. The majority of
chrysanthemums grown today are florists
chrysanthemums, hybrids of *Chrysanthemum
Morifolium*. These are half hardy annuals and
perennials. Leaves are usually deeply lobed or cut
and have a distinctive pungent scent. Flowers
occur in a wide variety of forms, from small, flat
daisy-like blooms to large spherical forms. Plants
vary in size from dwarf plants, producing
hundreds of tiny star-shaped flowers, to large
exhibition plants that have been disbudded to
produce a single huge bloom.

Flowering Period:	Early, mid and late autumn.
Cultivation:	Moist but well-drained, fertile soil in an open sunny site.
Propagation:	Annuals by seed in spring, perennials by division in autumn, after flowering, or in early spring.
Gardening tip:	Tall varieties require staking. Lift and store in a frost-free environment over winter.
Illustration:	*Chrysanthemum hybrid.*

Clarkia

Clarkia syn. *Godetia*   Onagraceae

Fully hardy, fast growing annual, slender
stemmed and leafy, with flower heads of double
or semi-double flowers in many shades of white,
mauve and pink, including salmon; leaves are
lance-shaped and mid-green. Popular as cut
flowers.

Flowering Period: Summer and early autumn.
Cultivation: In fertile, well-drained soil in a sunny spot.
Propagation: By seed sown outdoors in spring, or in early autumn in mild areas.
Gardening tip: Avoid too rich soil, as this encourages vegetation at the expense of flowers.
Illustration: *Clarkia.*

Clematis

Clematis   Ranunculaceae

One of the most popular of climbing plants,
although a few species are herbaceous,
unsurpassed in its long period of flowering.
Clematis can be evergreen or deciduous and is
fully to half hardy. Grown for its mass of often
showy flowers and decorative seedheads.
Clematis may be divided into three groups:
(1) Early flowering species, *Alpina, Macropetala*
and *Montana* types; (2) Early, large flowered
cultivars; (3) Late, large flowered cultivars and
herbaceous types.

Flowering Period:	There are early and late varieties, some will be in flower at almost any time.
Cultivation:	In rich, well-drained soil in shade or full sun, but prefers to have its roots in shade.
Propagation:	Some species from seed sown in autumn. Cultivars in early summer by softwood or semi-ripe cuttings or layering.
Gardening tip:	Very effective when trailing through or over other plants such as shrubs or even trees.
Illustration:	*Clematis* – late, large flowered cultivar.

Columbine

Aquilegia   Ranunculaceae

Graceful, ultra-hardy but short-lived, clump-forming perennials, with rounded, finely divided leaves and profuse, bell-shaped flowers. Sepals and petals are often in contrasting colours, petals extending back to form spurs.

Flowering Period: Spring and summer.
Cultivation: Well-drained soil with peat or leaf mould in open, sunny site.
Propagation: By seed in autumn and spring.
Gardening tip: Very good for rock gardens.
Illustration: *Aquilegia alpina* (Alpine columbine).

Cornflower
(also Knapweed)

Centaurea   Compositae

Fully hardy, fast growing annuals and perennials,
in many shades of blue, mauve, pink and yellow.
Popular in borders and as cut flowers. Flower
heads have thistle-like centres surrounded by
rings of narrow petals.

Flowering Period: Summer and early autumn.
Cultivation: In any soil that is well-drained,
                      in full sun.
Propagation: By seed or division in spring
                      or autumn.
Gardening tip: Very easy to grow, even in
                      poor soil.
Illustration: *Centaurea cyanus* (Cornflower).

Cosmos

Cosmos   Compositae

Fully to half hardy annuals and tuberous
perennials. Annuals are moderately fast growing,
erect and bushy plants, mostly tall with elegant,
mainly single, flowers ideal for the backs of
borders and for cutting.

Flowering Period: Summer and early autumn.
Cultivation: In moist but well-drained soil
                        in full sun.
Propagation: Annuals by seed in spring or
                        autumn, half hardy species by
                        basal cuttings in spring.
Gardening tip: Dead-head to prolong
                        flowering period.
Illustration: *Cosmos* "Sensation".

Cranesbill

Geranium — Geraniaceae

Clump-forming perennials, fully to half hardy.
Grown for their attractive, often finely veined
saucer-shaped flowers in many shades of blue,
pink and purple to deep maroon. Leaves are
deeply cut or lobed. Compact species are suitable
for rock gardens and ground covering, taller
plants for borders.

Flowering Period:	Early to mid-summer.
Cultivation:	In any well-drained soil. Most species prefer sun but some are better in shade.
Propagation:	By seed or division in spring or autumn. Cultivars by division or cuttings only.
Gardening tip:	Cut back taller species after flowering.
Illustration:	*Geranium wallichianum* "Buxton's Blue".

Crinum

Crinum   Amaryllidaceae

Robust bulbs, frost-hardy to frost-tender, grown for their stately funnel-shaped flowers carried on tall, leafless stems rising above a tangle of strap-like leaves. Crinum provides a dramatic contrast to plants with rounded foliage.

Flowering Period: Late summer to autumn.
Cultivation: Needs a sheltered position in full sun and rich, well-drained soil.
Propagation: By seed or offsets in spring.
Gardening tip: Crinum is luxuriant and needs plenty of space.
Illustration: *Crinum powelli.*

Crocus

Crocus   **Iridaceae**

Hardy and among the most popular and colourful
of corms. Funnel-shaped flowers, often opening
to starry- or cup-shaped, in white, yellow, pink
and purple, grow close to the ground, with
narrow, semi-erect leaves, often with a silvery
line along the centre. Some autumn flowering
species have no leaves at flowering time, these
following in winter or spring. They look
beautiful scattered amongst grass under trees and
shrubs, and are also good for rock gardens and
containers.

Flowering Period: Spring or autumn.
Cultivation: In well-drained soil in sun or
light shade.
Propagation: In early autumn by seed or
cormlets.
Gardening tip: Do not mow grass which has
been planted with crocus until
the leaves turn yellow.
Illustration: *Crocus vernus* (Spring crocus).

Cyclamen

Cyclamen   **Primulaceae**

Tuberous perennials, fully hardy to frost-tender
shade-lovers forming carpets of heart-shaped
leaves which are often blotched or marbled silver.
Flowers have five turned-back petals in shades of
white, pink, crimson and violet, often with a
mouth stained in a darker colour.

Flowering Period: Generally late winter to early
spring, but some varieties
flower in summer or autumn.

Cultivation: In well-drained peaty soil in
full or partial shade. Excellent
for underplanting shrubs and
trees, walls and shady rock
gardens; can also be
pot-grown.

Propagation: By seed in late summer or
early autumn.

Gardening tip: For pot-grown plants, dry off
tubers in summer, re-pot in
autumn and water to restart
growth.

Illustration: *Cyclamen vernum* (Winter/early
spring flowering).

Daffodil

Narcissus   **Amaryllidaceae**

Fully hardy bulbs for naturalizing in grass, for
borders, bedding and containers, and for cut
flowers. The charm and diversity of daffodils,
from the tiniest wild forms to the stately trumpet
daffodil makes it one of the most popular of
garden plants. Horticulturally, *narcissus* is split
into twelve divisions. The following description
refers specifically to daffodils. Each flower has a
trumpet (the corona) surrounded by petals. Often
the trumpet is deep yellow and the petals lighter
yellow, but some are evenly coloured
throughout, yellow or white, or have an orange-
yellow trumpet surrounded by white petals.
Leaves are strap-shaped and bluish-green.

Flowering Period:	Spring.
Cultivation:	In well-drained soil in sun or light shade.
Propagation:	Fresh seed in late summer or autumn. Most cultivars increase naturally by offsets.
Gardening tip:	Foliar-feed plants. Dead-head, but do not cut or tie leaves until dead. Divide crowded clumps in mid-summer. Best grown in grass which is unmown until leaves die down.
Illustration:	*Trumpet daffodil.*

Dahlia

Dahlia   Compositae

Half hardy tuberous perennials, dahlia hybrids
occur in a spectacular range of colour and flower
forms, from the miniature pompons to giant
exhibition blooms of one foot or more across.
There are at least ten groups of flower forms.
Colours range from white, cream and pastel
shades of pink and lilac, to vibrant pinks, reds,
purples and bronze. They are widely used as cut
flowers as well as for making a dazzling display
in the garden.

Flowering Period: Late summer to autumn.
Cultivation: In borders, containers and beds in rich, well-drained but moist soil in the sun. All but the smallest types require staking.
Propagation: By seed in spring, or by basal shoot cuttings or division of tubers.
Gardening tip: Plants may be left in the ground in mild areas, but surface shoots should always be cut by the first frosts of autumn.
Illustration: Single Dahlia of "miscellaneous" form, ie not conforming to a specifically named flower shape.

Day lily

Hemerocallis   ### Liliaceae

Fully hardy perennials, some of which are
evergreen. Flowers, in colours ranging from pale
cream and yellow through peach and rose to red,
purple and maroon, are borne in succession, each
lasting for only a day. Leaves are strap-like and
glossy. Good for herbaceous and mixed borders.

Flowering Period: Late spring to midsummer.
Cultivation: In dry or moist soil in sun or
partial shade.
Propagation: By division in spring or
autumn.
Gardening tip: Divide after only five or six
years. Hemerocallis forms
totally weed-excluding ground
cover.
Illustration: *Hemerocallis x hybrida.*

Delphinium

Delphinium   Ranunculaceae

Fully to half hardy perennials and annuals.
Mainly tall and predominantly blue-flowering,
delphinium is a graceful border plant, with
racemes of irregularly cup-shaped, sometimes
hooded, spurred flowers. Colours include white,
pale yellow, dusky pink, mauve and purple as
well as the many shades of blue.

Flowering Period: All summer.
Cultivation: In deep, rich, moist but well-drained soil in an open sunny position.
Propagation: By seed or division in spring or autumn. Some species can be propagated by division or basal cuttings in spring.
Gardening tip: Tall varieties need staking. To promote a second flush of flowers in late summer, remove flower heads after they fade.
Illustration: *Delphinium* "Blue Nile".

English daisy

Bellis   Compositae

Very hardy, slow growing, mat-forming
perennials, some grown as biennials. Relative of
the lawn weed. Use for bedding, edging and
ground cover. Large-flowered and small-flowered
forms of the plant are available, some with
double flower heads. Leaves are oval and
mid-green.

Flowering Period: Spring.
Cultivation: In any well-drained soil in full
                      or partial sun.
Propagation: By seed in early summer or by
                      division after flowering.
Gardening tip: Pinch out growing tips to
                      promote bushy growth. Dead-
                      head regularly.
Illustration: *Bellis perennis.*

Evening primrose

Oenothera   Onagraceae

Very hardy herbaceous perennial admired for its profuse but short-lived flowers. The large, delicate, yellow cup-shaped flowers are borne in succession throughout the summer. Some flower at sunset and others are day flowering. Stems are prostrate and spreading and others clump-forming. Large species are suitable for wild gardens and borders, smaller ones for rock gardens and dry slopes in full sun.

Flowering Period: All summer.
Cultivation: In well-drained, even poor, soil.
Propagation: By seed or division in spring or autumn or by softwood cuttings in late spring.
Gardening tip: Water freely in dry weather.
Illustration: *Oenothera missouriensis* (Evening primrose).

Forget-me-not

Myosotis   Boraginaceae

Fully hardy annuals, biennials and perennials
grown for their small pretty flowers, which are
usually blue but occasionally pink, some with a
creamy white "eye" at the centre. Most species
are good for rock gardens and banks and there is
one (*Myosotis scorpioides*) that is grown as a
marginal water plant.

Flowering Period:	Late spring and early summer.
Cultivation:	In fertile, well-drained soil in sun or semi-shade.
Propagation:	By seed in autumn.
Gardening tip:	A very good plant for associating with spring bulbs.
Illustration:	*Myosotis alpestris* (Alpine forget-me-not).

Foxglove

Digitalis   Scrophulariaceae

Fully to frost hardy, slow growing biennials and
perennials, some of which are evergreen. Tall and
stately, with racemes of drooping tubular flowers
of rose-mauve, white, coppery or creamy-yellow
above a rosette of basal leaves. Good in borders
or for cutting. *Digitalis purpurea* grows prolifically
in the wild.

Flowering Period: Summer.

Cultivation: In rich but well-drained soil in partial shade.

Propagation: By seed in autumn. *Digitalis* will also self-seed.

Gardening tip: When growing white forms of *D. purpurea*, weed out common purple ones, as purple colouring is dominant and will eventually take over from the white.

Illustration: *Digitalis purpurea* (common foxglove of Europe).

Freesia

Freesia   **Iridaceae**

Half hardy corms, appreciated for their usually
fragrant flowers, which are very popular for
cutting. Flowers occur in one-sided arching
spikes on wiry stems, single and double forms in
a wide colour range from white and yellow to
pink, red, orange and purple. Bright green leaves
are sparse and erect in basal fans.

Flowering Period: Winter and spring.
Cultivation: In well-drained soil in full sun.
                       Plant in autumn and water
                       throughout the winter.
Propagation: By seed in spring or offsets in
                       winter.
Gardening tip: Provide support of twigs or
                       small canes.
Illustration: *Freesia* hybrid.

Fritillary

Fritillaria   **Liliaceae**

Fully to frost-hardy bulbs producing bell-shaped
flowers in unusual shades of blackish to brownish
purple, red-violet, olive green to greenish yellow
and green tinged white, while in many cases
chequered or streaked with contrasting colours.
Flowers are sometimes borne singly on slender
stems and sometimes occur as racemes. Leaves are
generally narrow and grey-green. Suitable for
naturalizing in grass, underplanting trees and
shrubs and for containers.

Flowering Period:	Spring.
Cultivation:	In well-drained soil that dries out in summer but does not become sunbaked, in full sun or partial shade.
Propagation:	By seed in autumn or winter, or by offsets in summer.
Gardening tip:	*Fritillary meleagris* is particularly good for naturalizing in grass. It needs moisture-retentive soil.
Illustration:	*Fritillaria meleagris* (Snake's head fritillary).

Fuchsia

Fuchsia   Onagraceae

Frost-hardy to frost-tender evergreen or
deciduous shrub grown for their flowers. Shrubs
may be large and bushy with many small flowers
to smaller plants with large flowers. Pendulous,
tubular flowers have spreading/reflexing petals
and are often bicoloured, with a bell-shaped
corolla and protruding stamens and pistil.

Flowering Period: Early summer to early autumn.
Cultivation: In sun or light shade in a
sheltered position, in well-
drained, moist and fertile soil.
Large varieties suitable for
hedging and screening, smaller
ones for containers and
bedding.
Propagation: By softwood cuttings in any
autumn.
Gardening tip: Water frequently in dry
weather. Plants used for
summer bedding require
staking.
Illustration: *Fuchsia* hybrid

Gentian

Gentiana   Gentianaceae

Generally hardy annuals, biennials and perennials,
they are grown for their usually blue flowers.
Among the most well-known groups of alpine
and rock garden plants. Some are evergreen or
semi-evergreen, with narrow toothless and often
stalkless leaves. Flowers are bell-shaped or long-
tubed and starry, and generally five-lobed.

Flowering Period: Different species and varieties
flower in spring, summer and
autumn.

Cultivation: Needs vary, but generally in
humus-rich, moist, well-
drained soil in sun or
semi-shade.

Propagation: By seed in autumn or by
division or offshoots in spring.

Gardening tip: Good for slightly acid soils.
Some species grow naturally in
limestone soils.

Illustration: *Gentiana verna* (Spring gentian).

Geranium

Pelargonium   ## Geraniaceae

Frost-tender perennials, most of which are evergreen, grown for their flowers and scented leaves. Generally very free-flowering, in warm conditions almost continuously. They are mainly adaptable and tolerant and are very popular in containers or beds. Single and double flowers occur in shades of pink, white, red, orange and purple, and some have variegated and/or scented leaves. *Pelargoniums* are purple, and some have variegated and/or scented leaves. *Pelargoniums* are divided into four groups: (1) Zonal – the common geranium, with single to double flowers and rounded leaves distinctively marked with a darker "zone"; (2) Regal – shrubby plants with large, exotic flowers and deeply scented leaves; (3) Ivy-leaved – trailing plants with single to double flowers and fleshy leaves, ideal for hanging baskets; (4) Scented-leaved and species – grown for their fragrant leaves. Plants have small, often star-shaped flowers.

Flowering Period:	Mainly summer.
Cultivation:	In well-drained soil in full sun, but it dislikes very hot, humid conditions. Daylight is an important requirement – twelve hours for good flowering.
Propagation:	By softwood cuttings from spring to autumn.
Gardening tip:	Dead-head frequently; fertilize regularly if kept in pots.
Illustration:	*Zonal pelargonium.*

Geum

Geum   **Rosaceae**

Fully hardy clump-forming perennial, with strongly coloured single or double rosette flowers borne on slender, branching stems. Compound leaves are fresh green and hairy with usually rounded and lobed leaflets. Geums are mostly popular for borders, but some of the smaller ones are suitable for rock gardens.

Flowering Period: All summer.
Cultivation: In moist but well-drained soil in the sun.
Propagation: By seed or division in autumn.
Gardening tip: Mulch in spring.
Illustration: *Geum borisii.*

Gladiolus

Gladiolus   Iridaceae

Semi-hardy corm; very tall erect plant with
spikes of showy, trumpet-shaped flowers in a
wide range of colours, including white, yellows,
pinks, reds and purples as well as bicolours.
Leaves are erect and spear-like. They are grown
extensively for cut flowers and exhibition.

Flowering Period:	Generally summer, but different varieties bloom early, mid and late season.
Cultivation:	In well-drained fertile soil in the sun, in mixed and herbaceous borders.
Propagation:	Propagation of named varieties by corm.
Gardening tip:	Need to be lifted before the first frost and kept in frost-free conditions over winter.
Illustration:	Variety of *Gladiolus grandiflorus*.

Globe flower

Trollius   ### Ranunculaceae

Fully hardy, moisture loving, clump-forming
perennial. Globe-shaped flowers, generally yellow
to orange but occasionally yellowish-white, are
like large incurved buttercups. Leaves are deeply
lobed.

Flowering Period:	Late spring to early summer.
Cultivation:	Does best in moist soil; tolerates sun or shade.
Propagation:	By seed in summer or autumn, or division in early autumn.
Gardening tip:	*Trollius* thrives beside pools and streams.
Illustration:	*Trollius x hybrida.*

Globe thistle

Echinops   Compositae

Ultra-hardy erect perennials, with globular,
prickly, metallic-blue heads and large, deeply
serrated leaves. *Echinops* are tall, bushy, and in
some cases massive, plants and need plenty of
space at the back of a border or bed.

Flowering Period: Summer.
Cultivation: In poor soil in full sun.
Propagation: By seed or division in autumn
or by root cuttings in winter.
Gardening tip: The flower-heads can be dried
and used for flower
arrangements.
Illustration: *Echinops ritro.*

Glory-of-the-snow

Chionodoxa   Liliaceae

Fully hardy bulb producing clustered, wide open
starry flowers, generally blue or pink with a
white eye, on leafless stems. Basal leaves are
semi-erect and narrow or curved. Suitable for
rock gardens and naturalizing in wild gardens and
under shrubs. Good for cutting.

Flowering Period:	Very early spring.
Cultivation:	In well-drained soil in sun or partial shade, *Chionodoxa* is less tolerant of damp shade than other similar species.
Propagation:	By seed in autumn or by division in late summer or autumn.
Gardening tip:	Top-dress with leaf mould or mature garden compost in autumn.
Illustration:	*Chionodoxa luciliae*, syn. *Chionodoxa gigantea*.

Grape hyacinth

Muscari   **Liliaceae**

Fully to half hardy dwarf bulbs, with leafless
flower stems bearing dense spikes of small,
globular flowers, generally blue but occasionally
white or pale yellow, with a cluster of narrow,
strap-shaped basal leaves. The leaves usually
appear in spring just before the flowers. Ideal for
rock gardens, borders and containers.

Flowering Period: Spring to late spring.
Cultivation: In any well-drained soil,
preferably in the sun.
Propagation: Plant seed or bulbs in autumn,
or propagate by division in late
summer.
Gardening tip: *Muscari* multiplies freely and is
therefore excellent for
naturalizing.
Illustration: *Muscari neglectum*, syn. *muscari
racemosum* (Musk hyacinth).

Gypsophila
(also Chalk Plant, Baby's Breath)

Gypsophila   Caryophyllaceae

Fully hardy annuals and perennials, some of which are evergreen. Bushy, airy plants with drifts of generally tiny white to pink flowers borne on wiry, branching stems. Gypsophila is very popular as a cut flower, its fine cloud-like sprays making a perfect foil to heavier flowers. Similarly in borders it contrasts well with heavy-leaved perennials.

Flowering Period:	Spring to autumn.
Cultivation:	Will grow in dry, sandy and stony soils in the sun, but does best in deep, well-drained soil.
Propagation:	By seed in spring or autumn, or by softwood cuttings in summer.
Gardening tip:	Does not like being disturbed. Cut back after flowering for a second flush of flowers.
Illustration:	*Gypsophila paniculata.*

Heather

Heather also *Heath*   Ericaceae

Fully hardy to frost-tender shrubs, woody
stemmed and evergreen, heathers vary in habit
from dwarf, prostrate forms to tree-heaths up to
twenty-feet high. There are three genera: *Calluna,
Daboecia* and *Erica,* of which the largest genus is
Erica. Heathers are very popular for ground
covering and for rock gardens. The huge range of
plants available offers colour all the year round.
Carpets of purple heather are a familiar sight in
wild moorland areas.

Flowering Period:	Some species in flower at any time of year.
Cultivation:	In peaty, well-drained soil in an open sunny position.
Propagation:	Species by seed in spring or by layering, softwood cuttings or division in summer. Cultivars should be vegetatively propagated.
Gardening tip:	Some species are too vigorous for small rock gardens and may swamp smaller plants unless cut back often. In any case cut back lightly after flowering each year to promote compact and bushy habit.
Illustration:	*Erica cinerea* (Bell Heather).

Himalayan Blue Poppy
(and relatives)

Meconopsis   Papaveraceae

Fully hardy perennials grown for their beautiful
flowers, some of which are short-lived and others
monocarpic (die after flowering). The genus
includes the native Welsh poppy M. Cambrica.
Leaves are often deeply cut and hairy. *Meconopsis*
species includes flowers that are pale lemon to
deep rich yellow, orange and red, besides blues.
The flowers, of typical poppy shape, are mostly
large and often silky or crepe-like.

Flowering Period: Late spring to early summer.
Cultivation: In humus-rich, moist soil in a
                      cool, shady site.
Propagation: By seed in late summer or
                      division after flowering.
Gardening tip: Divide every two to three
                      years to maintain vigour.
Illustration: *Meconopsis grandis.*

Hollyhock

Alcea   Malvaceae

Ultra-hardy biennials and short-lived perennials.
Tall, erect stems carry spikes of pink, yellow,
cream, magenta or deep red-purple single or
double flowers, with often prominent stamens.
Leaves are lobed and rough textured. Best
position for *alcea* is against a sheltered wall or at
the rear of a border.

Flowering Period: Summer to early autumn.
Cultivation: In rich, well-drained soil in full sun.
Propagation: By seed in late spring or summer.
Gardening tip: Support exposed plants by staking.
Illustration: *Alcea rosea*, syn. *Alathea rosea*.

Honesty

Lunaria annua   **Cruciferae**

Fully hardy biennials and perennials grown for
their silvery, disc-shaped seed-pods that are
popular for dried flower arrangements.

Flowering Period:	Flowers in spring and early summer followed by seed-pods in autumn.
Cultivation:	In well-drained soil. Tolerates sun but prefers shade.
Propagation:	Perennials by seed in spring or autumn, or by division in spring. Biennials by seed only. Self-seeds prolifically.
Gardening tip:	Seeds need to be removed from pods to achieve full, silvery translucency for indoor decoration.
Illustration:	*Lunaris annua*, syn. *Lunaria biennis* (Honesty).

Honeysuckle

Lonicera   Caprifoliaceae

Woody-stemmed, twining climbers and shrubs
that may be deciduous, semi-evergreen or evergreen and are fully hardy to frost-tender. Grown
for their whorls of tubular, often superbly fragrant
flowers. Climbers are at their best rambling over
bushes and pergolas and are very useful for
disguising unsightly and immovable objects in the
garden such as old tree stumps or boring walls.

Flowering Period:	Early summer to autumn, some shrubby species in winter.
Cultivation:	In any fertile well-drained soil in sun or semi-shade, but like to have cool, moist roots.
Propagation:	By seed in spring or autumn, by semi-ripe cuttings in summer or by hardwood cuttings in late autumn.
Gardening tip:	Prune out flowered wood of climbers after flowering. Prune shrubs only to remove dead shoots or restrain growth. Climbers may be trained into large shrubs.
Illustration:	*Lonicera periclymenun* (Common honeysuckle)

Hyacinth

Hyacinthus   Liliaceae

Frost-hardy bulbs, one of the most popular
harbingers of spring, both in the garden and as pot
plants indoors. Specially treated bulbs of *Hyacinthus
orientalis* cultivars can be potted in autumn for
forcing to produce flowers in mid-winter. Dense
spikes of fragrant, tubular flowers with reflexed
petals are borne on strong, leafless stems. The most
popular colours are the white-pink-blue range, but
cream, yellow, apricot, orange and red are also
available. Glossy, strap-shaped, semi-erect basal
leaves develop fully only after flowering.

Flowering Period:	Spring, or winter for forced potted plants indoors.
Cultivation:	In any well-drained soil in full sun, in beds or containers. Small species are good for rock gardens (see Grape hyacinth).
Propagation:	By offsets in late summer or early autumn.
Gardening tip:	After forcing, keep plants that have been grown indoors in a cool place to finish growth, then plant out to recover.
Illustration:	*Hyacinthus orientalis.*

Ice plant

Lampranthus   **Aizoaceae**

Creeping, bushy perennial succulents and sub-shrubs with fleshy cylindrical to three-sided leaves and satiny, daisy-like flowers in brilliant yellows, pinks, magentas or purples, which only open in sunshine or bright daylight. Relatives of the mesembryanthemum. Semi-hardy but definitely frost-tender. Good for rock gardens, containers and ground cover, particularly in arid conditions.

Flowering Period: All summer.
Cultivation: In very well-drained, even sandy soil in full sun.
Propagation: By seed or by stem cuttings in spring or autumn.
Gardening tip: Resistant to drought and good for sand stabilization. Particularly suited to coastal gardens.
Illustration: *Lampranthus spectabilis.*

Iris

Iris   Iridaceae

Fully hardy rhizomatous or bulbous perennials.
Originally named after Iris, the Greek goddess
associated with the rainbow, these beautiful and
distinctive flowers are borne upon upright, leafless
stems and surrounded by erect, spear-like leaves,
usually in a basal fan. Irises occur in many forms,
which are variously suited to borders, rock gardens,
woodland, waterside and bog gardens, containers,
alpine houses and cold frames. Botanically, irises
are divided into a number of Subgenera and
Sections. The vast majority of irises grown in
gardens occur in the category "Bearded Irises",
which have ruffled flowers with a beard of fleshy
hairs on the lower "fall" petals. The following
information applies specifically to this group.

Flowering Period: Spring and early summer.
Cultivation: Bearded Irises need dry
                      conditions. Most others thrive in
                      moist or even boggy conditions.
Propagation: Plant firmly, leaving top of
                      rhizome exposed, in winter.
Gardening tip: Divide rhizomes every three to
                      four years after flowering.
                      Discard woody centre.
Illustration: *Bearded Iris.*

Jasmine

Jasminum officinale   Oleaceae

Deciduous or evergreen shrubs and woody-stemmed, scrambling or twining climbers, fully hardy to frost-tender. The small starry flowers, often sweetly scented, are mainly white or yellow. Good for training on walls, trellises, pergolas and elsewhere.

Flowering Period:	Early to late summer, also winter, for different varieties.
Cultivation:	In fertile, well-drained soil in full sun or light shade.
Propagation:	By semi-ripe cuttings in summer.
Gardening tip:	No regular pruning needed, but thin out old shoots after flowering.
Illustration:	*Jasminum officinale* (common jasmine).

Jonquil

Narcissus   **Amaryllidaceae**

Jonquils are one of the divisions of the narcissus or daffodil family (described separately). Fully hardy bulbs for naturalizing in grass, for borders and for bedding, the flowers are sweetly scented and very popular for cutting as well as in the garden. Each flower has a cup (the corona) which is short and orange, surrounded by rounded, often flat yellow or white petals.

Flowering Period: Spring.
Cultivation: In well-drained soil in sun or light shade.
Propagation: By fresh seed in late summer or autumn. Most cultivars increase naturally by offsets.
Gardening tip: Foliar-feed plants. Dead-head, but do not cut or tie leaves until dead. Divide in mid-summer.
Illustration: Jonquil.

Kaffir lily

Schizostylis   **Iridaceae**

Frost-hardy, rhizomatous perennials for borders;
excellent for cutting. Starry, cup-shaped pale pink
to crimson flowers are borne in erect spikes
above narrow, strap-shaped leaves.

Flowering Period:	All through autumn.
Cultivation:	In fertile, moist soil in a sunny and sheltered position.
Propagation:	By division in spring.
Gardening tip:	Mulch in winter in cold areas and divide clumps every three or four years in the spring, as they rapidly become congested.
Illustration:	*Schizostylis coccinea* (Kaffir lily).

Lady's mantle

Alchemilla   Rosaceae

Fully hardy clump-forming perennial grown mainly for ground cover and dry banks; is also used as cut flowers. Sprays of tiny, greenish-yellow flowers are surrounded by conspicuous outer calyces. *Alchemilla* is very attractive after rain, when drops lodge in the leaves.

Flowering Period: Mid-summer.
Cultivation: In any but boggy soil, in sun or partial shade.
Propagation: By seed or division in spring or autumn.
Gardening tip: Flowers may be dried for the winter.
Illustration: *Alchemilla mollis.*

Lily-of-the-valley

Convallaria   Liliaceae

Ultra-hardy rhizomatous perennials. Gracefully drooping sprays of small, very fragrant, bell-shaped flowers, waxy white or occasionally pink, arise between paired deep green leaves. Very good for ground cover or in a woodland garden, and for cutting.

Flowering Period: Spring.
Cultivation: In any soil but does best in humus-rich, moist soil, in sun or partial shade.
Propagation: By division after flowering or in autumn.
Gardening tip: Flowers are best pulled, not cut, when taken for indoors.
Illustration: *Convallaria majalis.*

Lily

Lilium   Liliaceae

Frost-hardy bulbs, which produce tall, stately plants with elegant and often very fragrant flowers. Leafy stems are crowned with flat or reflexing trumpet-shaped flowers in a wide spectrum of colours from white through cream, pink and orange, to ruby and purplish red, generally spotted inside. They are ideal plants for borders and are very good for cutting.

Flowering Period:	All summer.
Cultivation:	Any well-drained soil in the sun.
Propagation:	By seed in spring or autumn, bulb scales in summer or stem bulbils in autumn.
Gardening tip:	If soil is heavy, plant deeply in a pocket of sand.
Illustration:	*Lilium rubrum magnificum.*

Lobelia

Lobelia   Campanulaceae

Half hardy annual, slow growing, compact and
spreading. Masses of tiny flowers in white, pink,
carmine, pale and deep sapphire blue; oval to
lance-shaped bronze or pale green leaves.

Flowering Period:	Continuously all summer and early autumn.
Cultivation:	Plant in well-drained soil in the sun. Small bushy varieties are popular for edging and rock gardens. Trailing varieties ideal for hanging baskets.
Propagation:	By seed in spring.
Gardening tip:	Dislikes wet conditions in winter. Remove to cold frame in autumn in cold areas.
Illustration:	*Lobelia erinus* (Edging lobelia).

Lords and ladies
(also Cuckoo pint and
Parson in the pulpit)

Arum   Araceae

Tuberous perennials with large, lush, ornamental leaves and flower-like spathes surrounding a fleshy spadix of insignificant true flowers, often followed by red or orange berries. Moderately to fully hardy; many grow wild in hedgerows.

Flowering Period:	Spathes appear in spring followed by leaves in autumn.
Cultivation:	Plant tubers four to six inches deep in moist but well-drained, humus-rich soil, in sun or partial shade.
Propagation:	By seed in autumn or division of offsets in early autumn.
Gardening tip:	A good plant for a woodland or wild garden, also favoured for flower arranging. If grown in open ground, lift tubers where not hardy and store in cool dry conditions over winter.
Illustration:	*Arum creticum.*

Love-in-a-mist

Nigella   **Ranunculaceae**

Fully hardy, fast growing annuals appreciated for
their attractive flowers and feathery foliage, and
for their ornamental seed-pods. Semi-double
flowers in shades of blue, pink or white arise
amidst a profusion of very finely divided, almost
thread-like leaves. Good for borders and beds and
a favourite flower for cutting.

Flowering Period: Summer.
Cultivation: In fertile, well-drained soil in
the sun.
Propagation: By seed in spring or early
autumn.
Gardening tip: Dead-head plants to prolong
flowering only if seed heads
are not required.
Illustration: *Nigella damascena.*

Lupin

Lupinus   Leguminosae

Group of annuals, perennials and semi-evergreen
shrubs. Garden lupins are mainly frost-hardy,
clump-forming perennials, grown for their large
racemes of pea-like flowers in many colours –
white, yellow, orange, red–purple and blue as
well as bicoloured, which rise above palmate,
deeply divided leaves. They are an imposing
presence in beds and borders.

Flowering Period: Early summer.
Cultivation: In well-drained soil in the sun.
Propagation: By seed in autumn or by
cuttings from non-flowering
side shoots in spring or early
summer.
Gardening tip: Remove seed heads to prevent
self-seeding.
Illustration: *Lupinus.*

Marguerite

Chrysanthemum **Compositae**

Marguerites are members of the chrysanthemum family, which is described earlier. The information on this page relates specifically to Marguerites.

Evergreen, woody-based, bushy perennial. Very hardy. Yellow-centred daisy-like flowers occur in yellow or pink, as well as the more familiar white, rising above fresh green, deeply cut leaves. A favourite plant for borders and beds.

Flowering Period: Late summer.
Cultivation: In dry, well-drained soil in full sun.
Propagation: By division in autumn, after flowering, or in early spring.
Gardening tip: Stake if plant becomes floppy. Divide regularly for healthy growth if grown in fertile soil.
Illustration: *Chrysanthemum frutescens*, syn. *Argyranthemum frutescens* (Marguerite).

Marigold

Calendula   Compositae

Fully hardy annuals and frost-tender shrubs. The
popular marigold for beds and borders is
Calendula officinalis (Pot marigold), of which there
are tall and dwarf forms. Daisy-like, single or
double flower heads are produced in cream or
apricot as well as the familiar vibrant orange;
leaves are pale green, lance-shaped and strongly
aromatic. Marigold petals make a colourful
addition to a summer salad as well as a bold
splash of colour in the garden.

Flowering Period:	Spring to autumn.
Cultivation:	In the sun in any well-drained soil.
Propagation:	Annuals by seed sown outdoors in spring or autumn, shrubs by stem cuttings in summer.
Gardening tip:	Dead-head to prolong flowering.
Illustration:	*Calendula officinalis* (Pot marigold).

Michaelmas daisy

Aster   Compositae

Michaelmas daisies are not botanically distinct
from other asters, which are described earlier.
The asters generally recognised as Michaelmas
daisies are hardy, upright perennials with small,
bluish to reddish purple daisy-like heads borne
upon tall branching stems with narrow, lance-
shaped leaves, popular for borders and cutting.

Flowering Period: Late summer to autumn.
Cultivation: In any fertile soil, moist and
                       well-drained, in the sun.
Propagation: By seed or softwood cuttings
                       in spring, or division in spring
                       or autumn.
Gardening tip: Michaelmas daisies can become
                       straggly. Stake tall plants and
                       divide them regularly.
Illustration: *Aster novi-belgii.*

Monkshood
(also Wolf's bane)

Aconitum   Ranunculaceae

Fully hardy perennials with poisonous tuberous
or fibrous roots. Hooded flowers, predominantly
in shades of blue and violet but also cream, are
borne on upright stems that are sometimes
scandent (loosely climbing). Leaves are generally
dark green, glossy and lobed. Good for borders,
rock gardens and woodland planting.

Flowering Period: Early to late summer.
Cultivation: In well-drained but deep,
                       moist soil in sun or partial
                       shade.
Propagation: By seed in autumn or division
                       in autumn every two or three
                       years.
Gardening tip: Shade enhances the colour of
                       the flowers.
Illustration: *Aconitum carmichaelii*
                       "Arendsii".

Montbretia

Crocosmia   Iridaceae

Very hardy corms which form dense clumps of sword-shaped erect leaves and arching sprays of yellow, orange or deep red funnel-shaped flowers. Good for borders or naturalizing in woodland gardens and for cutting. Grows prolifically in the wild in the south west.

Flowering Period: Summer.
Cultivation: In well-drained soil in an open sunny site.
Propagation: By division as growth commences in spring.
Gardening tip: Trim plant in spring. Protect in a cloche or similar in cold areas in the winter.
Illustration: *Crocosmia* "Citronella".

Morning glory

Ipomoea syn. *Pharbitis*
Convolvulaceae

Half hardy to frost-tender woody twining climbers, evergreen shrubs and perennials, with showy but short-lived trumpet-shaped flowers, mainly in the colour range red/purple/blue but occasionally white (*Ipomoea alba*, commonly Moonflower). They are cultivated relatives of bindweed. Best seen rambling over hedges, pergolas and walls, and excellent for temporary screening. Small varieties are suitable for ground cover.

Flowering Period:	Summer to early autumn.
Cultivation:	In humus-rich, well-drained soil in good light.
Propagation:	By seed in spring or by softwood cuttings in summer.
Gardening tip:	Thin out congested growth in spring. Dead-head to prolong flowering period. Water freely when in full growth.
Illustration:	*Ipomoea purpurea*, syn. *Convolvulus purpureus* (common Morning glory).

Nasturtium

Tropaeolum   Tropaeolaceae

Hardy annuals, perennials and twining climbers
grown for their funnel-shaped, spurred flowers in
vibrant shades of yellow, orange and red. Leaves
are very decorative, round or lobed and in many
cases edible; they add a peppery element to a
bland salad. Some have a trailing or prostrate
habit and are ideal for spilling over walls and
rockeries or in hanging baskets.

Flowering Period: Summer to autumn.
Cultivation: In poor, dry soil in the sun.
Propagation: By seed, tubers or basal stem-
cuttings in spring.
Gardening tip: All tropaeolums are best
treated as hardy annuals.
Illustration: *Tropaeolum majus* (garden
nasturtium).

Ornamental onion

Allium   Liliaceae

Fully to frost hardy perennials, with bulbs, rhizomes or fibrous rootstocks. Nearly all have narrow, basal leaves smelling of onions when crushed and have umbels of small flowers in shades of yellow, pink, mauve, blue or white. Tall varieties make a striking addition to borders and smaller ones look well in beds and containers.

Flowering Period:	Spring and summer.
Cultivation:	In well-drained soil in an open, sunny situation.
Propagation:	By seed in autumn or by division of clumps – spring-flowering varieties in late summer and summer-flowering ones in spring.
Gardening tip:	Best left undisturbed to form clumps. Dried umbels of tall species are good for winter decoration.
Illustration:	*Allium neapolitanum* syn. *Allium cowanii.*

Pansy
(*Viola wittrockiana*)

Viola   Violaceae

The viola family comprises perennials and
deciduous sub-shrubs, fully to half hardy. In
horticultural terms there is no distinction to be
made between pansies, violas and violets, but
since in popular terms these are recognised as
three separate plants they are featured separately.
Pansies are short-lived bushy perennials grown as
annuals or biennials with flat, five-petalled
asymmetrical flowers in myriad colours. Pansies
are immensely popular as summer bedding plants
and for window boxes and other containers.

Flowering Period:	Mostly summer, but there are varieties that flower from late autumn to spring in mild, sheltered sites.
Cultivation:	In moist, fertile soil in sun or light shade.
Propagation:	By seed sown according to flowering season, or by softwood cuttings in spring or autumn.
Gardening tip:	Dead-head to prolong flowering period.
Illustration:	*Viola wittrockiana.*

Passion flower

Passiflora   Passifloraceae

Strong half hardy climber, woody and tendrilled.
Can be evergreen or semi-evergreen. Grown for
its unique flowers, said to symbolize the
Crucifixion. Leaves are generally lobed. Some
species produce edible fruits.

Flowering Period: Summer to autumn.
Cultivation: In a warm and sheltered
position where the soil is
fertile and well-drained. The
stems require support; a mesh
trellis against a wall is ideal for
this.
Propagation: By seed in spring or semi-ripe
cuttings in summer.
Gardening tip: Thin out crowded growth in
spring and remove dead flower
heads to encourage prolific
flowering.
Illustration: *Passiflora caerulea* (common blue
Passion flower).

Peace lily

Spathyllum   Araceae

Tufted evergreen perennials with rhizomes; frost-tender. Grown for their ornamental foliage and dramatic white flowers. Glossy leaves are lance-shaped, semi-erect and mid to dark green. Intermittently bears oval, white spathes enclosing fleshy white spadices of fragrant flowers.

Flowering Period:	Irregular – can occur at any time.
Cultivation:	In humus-rich, moist soil in partial shade.
Propagation:	By division in spring or summer.
Gardening tip:	Likes a humid atmosphere.
Illustration:	*Spathyllum wallisii* (Peace lily).

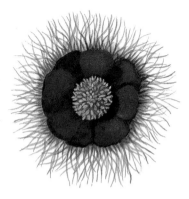

Peony

Paeonia   **Paeoniaceae**

Fully hardy perennials and deciduous shrubs (tree peonies). Peonies have been cultivated for many years, well loved for their bold foliage and beautiful, showy flowers. Peony flowers vary from single to double or anemone form (with broad outer petals and a mass of petaloids in the centre), in colours ranging from white through cream, yellow, pale to deep pinks and strong dark red. Very long-lived. Peonies are very good in beds and borders and as cut flowers.

Flowering Period:	Late spring and early to mid-summer.
Cultivation:	In rich, well-drained soil in full sun, although it will tolerate light shade.
Propagation:	By seed in autumn (may take three years to germinate). Perennials by division in early spring or autumn.
Gardening tip:	Water well in hot, dry weather; top-dress and mulch in autumn.
Illustration:	*Paeonia tenuifolia* (Fern-leaved peony).

Periwinkle

Vinca   Apocynaceae

Evergreen trailing sub-shrubs and perennials,
fully to frost-hardy. Glossy dark green leaves, in
some varieties edged with cream, form a
spreading, extensive mat studded with starry,
five-petalled, blue, purple or white flowers. Very
good for ground cover or trailing down the
hedge of a wild garden.

Flowering Period: Mid-spring to early summer.
Cultivation: In any moist soil in a shady
place, but flowers will grow
more freely if they have some
sun.
Propagation: By semi-ripe cuttings in
summer or by division from
autumn to spring.
Gardening tip: Is self-rooting and can be
invasive; keep well trimmed.
Illustration: *Vinca major*
(Greater periwinkle).

Petunia

Petunia   ### Solanaceae

Half hardy perennial; moderately fast growing
plant with showy funnel-shaped single or double
flowers, strongly veined, in all shades of blue,
purple, red, pink and white as well as bicolours.
Leaves are mid-green. Numerous varieties.

Flowering Period: All summer.
Cultivation: Treat as half hardy annuals.
                        Plant in rich soil in full sun in
                        a position sheltered from wind.
                        Some varieties are popular for
                        ground cover and others for
                        beds and containers.
Propagation: By seed sown under glass in
                        early spring.
Gardening tip: Dead-head regularly.
Illustration: Single petunia.

Phlox

Phlox **Polemoniaceae**

Very hardy, easily grown annuals and perennials, some of which are evergreen. Tall, erect species are popular as border plants; low growing alpine forms are favourite plants for rock gardens. Border phlox have showy, terminal panicles of flowers in a range of colours from white through pale pink, blue and mauve to deep purple, magenta and red. Rock phlox form cushiony mounds with a profusion of small, starry or saucer-shaped flowers, in a similar colour range, appearing amidst a mass of small oval or pointed leaves.

Flowering Period:	Late spring to late summer.
Cultivation:	In fertile, well-drained soil, in sun or partial shade.
Propagation:	By seed in spring or autumn or, for rock garden plants, by cuttings from non-flowering shoots in spring or summer.
Gardening tip:	Trim back rock garden species after flowering to promote compact habit.
Illustration:	*Phlox adsurgens.*

Pink

Dianthus   **Caryophyllaceae**

Pinks are smaller relatives of carnations. Fully to
half hardy evergreen, clump-forming perennials
with stems bearing four to six flowers rising
above a mass of narrow, lance-like grey leaves.
Flowers are fragrant and vary in form from single
to fully double. Pinks comprise two groups: Old
Fashioned, with a low, spreading habit and
producing one mass of flowers in mid-summer;
and Modern, which are more vigorous and produce
two or sometimes three flushes of flowers in one
season. Both groups are very good as border
decoration, in rock gardens and as cut flowers.

Flowering Period:	All summer.
Cultivation:	In well-drained, not too fertile soil in full sun.
Propagation:	By seed in spring or summer, or very easily by cuttings of non-flowering shoots, or layering, in summer.
Gardening tip:	Replace every two to three years, otherwise plants become too bushy. Narrow grey leaves make a good contrast to purple-leaved plants.
Illustration:	Modern pink.

Poppy
(True poppy)

Papavera   **Papaveraceae**

Fully hardy perennials with deep, fleshy roots.
Dramatic flowers with satiny or papery petals
and prominent stamens are carried on strong
stems. Broken stems and leaves exude acrid juice.
Flowers occur in single and double forms in
colours ranging from white, through salmon and
rose pink to blood red and vermilion, often
blotched with purplish black. Small, alpine species
are white or yellow. Leaves and stems are
generally hairy, mid green and deeply lobed, the
exception to this being *P. somniferum* (Opium
poppy) which has smooth, glaucous leaves and
stems. Large-flowered poppies make a spectacular
splash of colour in borders. The less showy
P. rhoeas (corn or field poppy) is a good subject
for a wild garden while *P. alpinum* (Alpine poppy)
is suitable for rock gardens.

Flowering Period:	All summer.
Cultivation:	Needs sun and moist but well-drained soil; although it will tolerate poor, dry soil.
Propagation:	By seed in spring and autumn; *P. orientale* by root cuttings in winter.
Gardening tip:	Foliage dies down in mid-summer; cut back hard to promote new growth. Flowers are cuttable if picked in bud and stems sealed in hot water.
Illustration:	*Papavera orientale.*

Potentilla

(Cinquefoil)

Potentilla   **Rosaceae**

Fully hardy perennials and small, dense,
deciduous shrubs, with peeling bark and showy,
saucer-shaped flowers in white, pale lemon to
deep yellow, orange and red. Small, deeply
divided leaves. Variously suited to borders, rock
gardens and for ground cover; taller varieties
make good hedges.

Flowering Period:	A long season from late spring to mid-autumn.
Cultivation:	In well-drained soil in the sun, but deeper coloured flowers benefit from being shaded from the hottest sun.
Propagation:	By seed in autumn or division in spring or autumn; shrubby species by seed or softwood cuttings in summer.
Gardening tip:	Occasionally thin out old shoots after flowering.
Illustration:	*Potentilla parvifolia.*

Primula

Primula   Primulaceae

Very large genus of annuals, biennials and
perennials, some of which are evergreen; fully
hardy to frost-tender. Most species have rosettes of
basal leaves and umbels of five-petalled flowers; a
few are clump-forming with flowers borne singly.
The leaves of many species are covered in farina,
a waxy powder. Botanically, *primulae* are classified
into thirty or more groups; for horticultural
purposes the main groups are: (1) *Candelabra*:
having tubular flowers in a series of umbels or
whorls up a tall stem. This group includes *P. veris*
(cowslip) which also grows in the wild.
(2) *Polyanthus*: Clump or rosette-forming with flat
flowers borne singly or in umbels. This group
includes *P. vulgaris* (common or wild primrose).
(3) *Auricula*: subdivided into Alpine, border and
show types. Flat flowers are borne in umbels.

There are primulas to suit almost every garden situation – waterside, wild areas and cool, moist rock gardens, while others thrive in more open sites in scree or alpine gardens and borders. Flowers of the *Candelabra* and *Polyanthus* groups occur in every shade of white, cream, pink and mauve to deep purple and maroon. Flowers of the *Auricula* group include, besides these, unusual colours such as grey and green, often with white or yellow centres and an outer ring in a contrasting colour.

Flowering Period: Spring to early summer.

Cultivation: Needs of different species vary considerably, but in general primulas require constant moisture and some shade.

Propagation: By seed in spring. Selected forms may be propagated during dormancy by division or root cuttings, *auriculas* by offsets in spring or early summer.

Gardening tip: Dead-head and tidy up foliage as flowering ceases. Grow show *auriculas* under glass to protect them from rain which would spoil their petals.

Illustration: *Primula vulgaris.*

Red-hot poker

(also Torch lily)

Kniphofia   Liliaceae or Aloeceae

Fully to half hardy perennials, some of which are evergreen. Dense terminal racemes of pendant tubular flowers are borne on stout stems rising from tufts of grassy or strap-shaped leaves. Not all flowers are orange or red as the popular name would imply; some are creamy or citron yellow tinged with green. They make good border plants.

Flowering Period: Early to late summer.
Cultivation: Best grown in full sun. All *Kniphofias* do well in coastal gardens.
Propagation: By seed or division in spring.
Gardening tip: In cold areas, protect the crowns with a winter mulch.
Illustration: *Kniphofia atlanta* (Red-hot poker).

Rock pink

Dianthus   Caryophyllaceae

Rock pinks are the smallest members of the *dianthus* family. Hardy, evergreen perennials with grassy, grey-green leaves forming tufted hummocks, they are attractive all the year round. A profusion of mainly single flowers in red, pink or white (rarely yellow) appears above the foliage. Excellent for dry walls, rock gardens and containers.

Flowering Period: All summer.
Cultivation: In well-drained soil in full sun.
Propagation: By seed in spring or summer, or very easily by cuttings of non-flowering shoots, or layering, in summer.
Gardening tip: Short-lived species best propagated every two to three years.
Illustration: *Dianthus alpinus* (Alpine pink).

Rose

Rosa   **Rosaceae**

Hardy shrub and scrambling climber. They are
officially classified in three groups: (1) Species and
Species hybrids, (2) Old and (3) Modern. Modern
is by far the largest group, in which plants occur
in many categories, ie shrub, bush, miniature,
ground covering, climbing and rambling, hybrid
tea and floribunda. The flowers occur in many
shapes, ranging from single flowers with only
four petals to fully double with over thirty petals.
Colours are every shade between white, cream
and salmon pink to vibrant magenta and deep
red, as well as bicoloured and striped. Leaves are
usually divided into leaflets with toothed edges
and stems usually bear thorns or prickles.

Flowering Period:	May to October.
Cultivation:	Roses prefer an open, sunny situation but can be grown in a variety of soils and conditions.
Propagation:	By budding in summer or hardwood cuttings in autumn.
Gardening tip:	Avoid planting in area where roses have been grown in recent years; exchange the soil or choose another site.
Illustration:	Modern climbing rose.

Rose of Sharon

(also Aaron's beard)

Hypericum   Hypericaceae

Generally hardy perennials, shrubs and sub-shrubs, grown for their conspicuous yellow flowers, which are sometimes followed by orange-red berries. Shrub species make very good ground cover, particularly under trees. The herbaceous species are commonly known as "St John's Wort".

Flowering Period:	Mid-summer to mid-autumn.
Cultivation:	Larger species need fertile, not too dry soil in sun or partial shade; smaller plants thrive best in full sun in very well-drained soil.
Propagation:	Perennials by seed or division in spring or autumn. Sub-shrubs and shrubs by softwood cuttings in summer, or seed in autumn.
Gardening tip:	Shrubby *Hypericum* grows vigorously and is self rooting; cut back hard in spring every few years.
Illustration:	*Hypericum calycinum* (Rose of Sharon).

Saxifrage

Saxifraga   Saxifragaceae

Fully to half hardy perennials, generally
evergreen. Stems are often wiry and sometimes
red. Flowers occur in red, white, yellow and
pink, sometimes spotted with red and having a
contrasting "eye". Saxifrage is botanically divided
into some fifteen sections encompassing a variety
of growing habits and cultivation requirements.
Three broad categories of the plant are generally
recognised horticulturally; these are: (1) Mossy,
(2) Encrusted or Silver (having lime on the leaves)
and (3) Cushion. There are other, uncategorized
species including taller varieties which are suitable
for borders as well as larger rock gardens.

Flowering Period:	Various species in spring, summer and autumn.
Cultivation:	Mostly require well-drained but moist soil in a cool, semi-shaded position; but some species need the sun and others need to be grown in an alpine house.
Propagation:	By seed in autumn or by rooted offsets in winter.
Gardening tip:	Many species benefit from from being divided and replanted every few years.
Illustration:	*Saxifraga burseriana* (cushion saxifrage).

Scabious

Scabiosa   Dispacaceae

Fully hardy, fast growing, upright bushy annual.
Slender stems carry scented flowers in shades of
blue, purple, red, pink or white, with
characteristic domed centres surrounded by
overlapping petals. Leaves are mid-green, lance-
shaped and lobed. There are tall and dwarf forms
of *scabiosa* suited respectively to borders and rock
gardens. Tall species are very good for cutting.

Flowering Period: Summer and early autumn.
Cultivation: In fertile, well-drained soil in
the sun.
Propagation: Annuals by seed in spring.
Perennials by basal cuttings in
summer, by seed in autumn or
by division in early spring.
Gardening tip: Stake tall varieties. Some
varieties resent disturbance and
should be grown in a spot
where they can be left in
peace.
Illustration: *Scabiosa atropurpurea*
(Pincushion flower).

Snapdragon

Antirrhinum   Scrophulariaceae

Perennials and semi-evergreen sub-shrubs usually
grown as annuals; fully to half hardy. Most
snapdragons grown in the garden are in the
group *A. majus*; an upright plant, branching from
the base. There is one trailing variety: *A. asarina*.
Flowers of all *antirrhinums* are two-lipped and not
spurred as are the related toadflaxes (*Linaria*), and
besides the well known "dragon's mouth" shape
occur in trumpet (*penstemon*) and tubular (*peloric*)
forms. Colours are white, red, purple and orange.
Popular for bedding and borders; the taller
varieties are good for cutting.

Flowering Period:	Spring to autumn.
Cultivation:	In rich, well-drained soil in the sun.
Propagation:	By seed in spring or early autumn.
Gardening tip:	Dead-head to prolong flowering season.
Illustration:	*Antirrhinum majus* (Snapdragon).

Snowdrop

Galanthus   **Amaryllidaceae**

Fully to frost-hardy bulbs. Pendant white flowers, which can be single or double, are borne singly on slender stems between two strap-shaped, generally glaucous leaves. Flowers have three large outer petals enclosing three small inner ones forming a cup which is marked in green. The plants form clumps and are ideal for planting in grass under deciduous trees; woodlands are their natural habitat. They are also good subjects for beds and containers and are good for cutting.

Flowering Period:	Mid-winter to early spring except for *G. reginae olgae* which is an autumn flowering variety.
Cultivation:	In moist, rich soil in partial shade.
Propagation:	By division in spring after flowering, or in late summer or autumn when bulbs are dormant.
Gardening tip:	Best planted in spring when plant is growing. Do not allow bulbs to dry out excessively while dormant.
Illustration:	*Galanthus nivalis* (common Snowdrop).

Spiderwort

Tradescantia   Commelinaceae

Hardy to frost-tender perennials, some of which
are evergreen. Plants occur in trailing, mat and
clump-forming, and erect forms. Most have
extremely decorative foliage and very small
flowers. Leaves are generally lance-shaped and
often striped or flushed in various shades of pink,
red, white, cream or purple. The three-petalled
flowers are pink, purple or white. Suitable for
sunny beds and borders; the trailing varieties are
specially good for hanging baskets and are
popular plants indoors as well as out.

Flowering Period:	In most cases intermittent but some species in summer.
Cultivation:	In fertile, moist soil in the sun.
Propagation:	Frost-tender species by tip cuttings, hardy species by division, in spring, summer or autumn.
Gardening tip:	Cut back or repropagate trailing species when they become straggly. Trailing and mat-forming plants can be trained to provide decorative cover over old walls, tree stumps and elsewhere.
Illustration:	*Tradescantia pallida* (Purple heart).

Spurge

Euphorbia   Euphorbiaceae

Shrubs, succulents and perennials, fully hardy to
frost-tender, grown for their showy heads of long
lasting bracts. The genus contains a number of plants
of varying forms, including the species commonly
known as poinsettia and the strange gingham golf
ball (*E. obesa*). The following description relates to
the plant generally recognised as spurge.

Flower heads consist of cup-shaped bracts, often
sulphurous greenish-yellow (but in the case of
E. griffithii orange-red), surrounding insignificant
flowers. The bracts are borne in umbels, terminal
clusters or in loosely crowded racemes, on
unbranched fleshy stems which also bear a mass of
lance-shaped leaves. Spurge is popular in borders
as a foil to other more colourful plants,
particularly blue ones.

Flowering Period: Spring to early summer.

Cultivation: In moist but well-drained soil in sun or partial shade.

Propagation: By seed in spring or summer, or by division in spring or early autumn.

Gardening tip: Plants exude irritant and often poisonous sap when cut; careful handling is required.

Illustration: *Euphorbia characia.*

Squill

Scilla   Liliaceae

Fully to half hardy bulbs with narrow leaves in basal clusters and racemes or umbels of starry, bell-shaped flowers in shades of blue ranging from the palest, hardly more than white, to deep, rich hyacinth. The plants are quite small and are very well suited to naturalizing in grass – in the wild they grow profusely in the short grass on cliff-tops.

Flowering Period: Mainly spring and summer.
Cultivation: In humus-rich, moist but well-drained soil in an open site in sun or partial shade.
Propagation: By seed in autumn or by division in late summer.
Gardening tip: Scilla spreads very freely; allow it some space and take care that it does not invade the space allocated to other plants.
Illustration: *Scilla siberica* (Squill).

Stephanotis

Stephanotis   Asclepiadaceae

Woody-stemmed, evergreen twining climber;
frost-tender, grown for its scented, waxy, white
flowers borne in small clusters amidst dark, glossy
leaves. A favourite flower for bridal bouquets.

Flowering Period: Spring to autumn.
Cultivation: In humus-rich, well-drained
soil with partial shade in
summer.
Propagation: By seed in spring or semi-ripe
cuttings in summer.
Gardening tip: Provide support such as trellis.
Trim overlong or crowded
stems in spring. Decrease
watering in cold weather.
Illustration: *Stephanotis floribunda.*

Stock

Matthiola   Cruciferae

Annuals, biennials, perennials and evergreen sub-shrubs, fully hardy to frost-tender. Flowers of most annuals and biennials are highly scented; some release their scent at night rather than during the day. Very popular plants for beds, borders and containers and are an essential plant for the traditional cottage garden; they are also very good as cut flowers. Most garden stocks are grown as annuals. Plants are fast growing, erect and bushy, with lance-shaped, glaucous leaves and long spikes of single or double flowers in white, cream, yellow, pink, red or purple.

Flowering Period: All summer.
Cultivation: In fertile, well-drained and ideally lime-rich soil in sun or partial shade.
Propagation: Annuals and biennials by seed in spring. Sub-shrubs by semi-ripe cuttings in summer.
Gardening tip: Tall cultivars may require support. Provide winter protection by placing cloche over plants grown as biennials.
Illustration: *Matthiola* (Stock).

Stonecrop

Sedum   Crassulaceae

Fully to frost-hardy annuals, biennials, perennials, shrubs and sub-shrubs, many of which are evergreen, with thick semi-prostrate stems and small succulent leaves which are often cylindrical, rounded or three-sided. Abundant starry, five-petalled flowers, in white, yellow or pink, are borne above the leaves, usually in umbels but sometimes singly. All *sedums* are appropriate for rock gardens.

Flowering Period: Summer.

Cultivation: In any well-drained, gritty soil (but does best in fertile soil) in full sun.

Propagation: By seed in spring or autumn, or by division or softwood cuttings of non-flowering shoots from spring to mid-summer.

Gardening tip: Very invasive; may succeed in very poor soil where all else has failed.

Illustration: *Sedum acre* (Biting Stonecrop).

Sunflower

Helianthus   **Compositae**

Fully hardy annuals and perennials, grown for
their huge, daisy-like flower heads. Mostly very
tall plants with single stems and large oval serrated
leaves, *helianthus* is a striking presence at the back
of a large border or against a sheltering wall.
Flowers are usually, but not invariably, yellow; a
few have creamy-white petals. All have large,
disc-like centres which can be brown, greenish
brown or purplish to black. Shorter, bushier
versions are available as well as the very tall
single-stemmed species. Sunflower seeds are edible
by both birds and humans.

Flowering Period:	Summer and autumn.
Cultivation:	In well-drained soil in the sun.
Propagation:	By seed or division in spring or autumn.
Gardening tip:	Tall species need staking.
Illustration:	*Helianthus annus.*

Sun rose

Helianthemum   Cistaceae

Evergreen spreading shrubs and sub-shrubs, fully
to frost hardy, grown for their profuse but short-
lived flowers. Leaves are small, narrow and softly
hairy, glaucous or dark green. Flowers, which
resemble small wild roses, occur in white, very
pale to deepest yellow, and pink, usually with a
deeper coloured centre; also in strong carmine
and flame red against which the stamens appear
bright yellow. Ideal for rock gardens and dry
banks.

Flowering Period: Spring to autumn.
Cultivation: In well-drained soil in full sun.
Thrives on lime.
Propagation: By semi-ripe cuttings in early
summer.
Gardening tip: Cut back lightly after
flowering to encourage a
succession of flowers.
Illustration: *Helianthemum* "Wisley Pink".

Sweet alyssum

(*Lobularia maritima*)

Lobularia   Cruciferae

Fully hardy dwarf annuals; fast growing bushy
plants with lance-shaped leaves and heads of tiny,
fragrant flowers in white, pink, purple or red.
Very popular for edging and beds, particularly
the white variety which is often used to
complement the deep blue of lobelias.

Flowering Period: Summer and early autumn.
Cultivation: In rich soil in full sun.
Propagation: By seed in late spring.
Gardening tip: Dead-head to encourage
                continuous flowering.
Illustration: *Lobularia maritima*
                (Sweet Alyssum).

Sweet pea

(*Lathyrus odoratus*)

Lathyrus   **Leguminosae**

Fragrant tendrilled climber, half hardy annual.
There are many species, including non-climbing
dwarf plants. The petals are often wavy, flowers
are in all shades of pink, mauve, magenta, red,
purple, white and cream. Leaves are oval and
mid-green.

Flowering Period:	All summer.
Cultivation:	All except dwarf varieties need support. Plant in well-drained, neutral or alkaline soil in full sun. Climbing varieties are good for screening, dwarf varieties for beds and borders; and for forming flowering hedges.
Propagation:	By seed (soaked before sowing) in early spring or early autumn.
Gardening tip:	Superb for cutting. Cut often to induce prolific flowering.
Illustration:	*Lathyrus odoratus* (Sweet Pea).

Thrift

Armeria   **Plumbaginaceae**

Fully to frost-hardy evergreen perennials and
occasionally sub-shrubs. Long lasting flowers are
borne in spherical umbels on stiff stems above
densely cushioned hummocks or loose rosettes of
narrow, pointed leaves. Flowers occur mostly in
shades of pink to deep ruby-red, but are
sometimes white. Good for rock gardens; also
popular as an edging plant. *A. maritima* grows
prolifically on cliff-tops and in rock crevices.

Flowering Period:	Late spring to early summer.
Cultivation:	In any well-drained soil in full sun.
Propagation:	By seed in autumn or by semi-ripe cuttings in summer.
Gardening tip:	All thrifts are very suitable for coastal gardens.
Illustration:	*Armeria maritima* (Sea pink).

Tobacco

(Flowering Tobacco)

Nicotiana   Solanaceae

Annuals and perennials, usually grown as annuals,
and semi-evergreen shrubs, frost-hardy to frost-
tender. Very popular as a border and bedding
plant and for cutting. Long, tubular starry
flowers in white, cream, pink, red, purple or
yellow are mostly fragrant, releasing their scent
on the night air. Leaves are long, rather rough
and mid-green.

Flowering Period:	All summer and early autumn.
Cultivation:	In fertile, well-drained soil.
Propagation:	Annuals and perennials by seed in early spring; shrubs by seed in spring or by semi-ripe cuttings in summer.
Gardening tip:	Needs sun but will tolerate shade.
Illustration:	*Nicotiana*, Domino Series.

Tree mallow

(*Lavatera arborea*)

Lavatera   Malvaceae

Semi-evergreen sub-shrub or shrub, tender to moderately hardy. Tall, bushy plants with wide, trumpet-shaped flowers in shades of white to rose pink and deep cerise, often with prominent stamens. Leaves are generally lobed, mid-green and sometimes downy. They are common on the coast of the British Isles. Good in wild gardens.

Flowering Period: All summer.
Cultivation: In light, well-drained soil, even in sand, in full sun.
Propagation: By seed in spring or early autumn, or by softwood cuttings in early spring or summer.
Gardening tip: Very easy to grow in coastal gardens.
Illustration: *Lavatera arborea* (tree mallow).

Tulip

Tulipa   **Liliaceae**

Fully hardy bulbs grown for their bold and
brilliant flowers. Tulips have a long history, most
famously in Holland where in the seventeenth
century many new varieties were cultivated,
changing hands for very large sums of money.
Prized specimens were often immortalized in
paintings by the most prestigious artists of the
period. Today, tulips are classified in fifteen
horticultural divisions. There are varieties to suit
any garden scheme, from the most formal to the
most riotous; including such diverse sites as beds,
borders, rock gardens and containers. They are
also amongst the most elegant of cut flowers.

   Single or double flowers are generally cup or
goblet-shaped and held upright on smooth stems,
with a few linear to lance-shaped leaves in mid to
blue-green borne on the stems. Flower colours
occur across the whole spectrum excluding blue;
many have stripes, edges or splashes of
contrasting colour.

Flowering Period: Early to late spring.
Cultivation: In well-drained soil in a sunny
                       position.
Propagation: By seed in spring or autumn,
                       or by division of bulbs in
                       autumn.
Gardening tip: Dead-head. In cool, wet areas
                       lift bulbs when leaves die
                       down and store in a dry place
                       for replanting in autumn.
Illustration: Single late tulip.

Valerian

Valeriana also *Centranthus*
Valerianaceae

Fully hardy perennials, suitable for borders and
rock gardens. Often naturalizes in wall crevices
and can be invasive. Loose clusters of tiny
flowers in white, pink or red are borne on
branched stems, with deeply cut greyish leaves.

Flowering Period: Late spring to autumn.
Cultivation: In any well-drained soil in a
sunny or even exposed site.
Propagation: By seed in spring or division
in autumn.
Gardening tip: *Valeriana officinalis* attracts cats;
to be avoided in a garden with
many neighbouring cats.
Illustration: *Centranthus ruber*
(Red Valerian).

Viola

Viola   Violaceae

Fully to half hardy, bushy perennials and smaller
relatives of pansies, violas are popular for borders
and path edging and for rock gardens.
Asymmetrical, five-petalled flowers in many
shades and colours, white, yellow, purple and
bronze, often blotched, bicoloured and even
tricoloured.

Flowering Period: Late spring to summer.
Cultivation: In moist but well-drained
                      fertile soil in cool semi-shade,
                      or in full sun where it is not
                      too hot.
Propagation: By seed in autumn or division
                      in spring.
Gardening tip: Dead-head and cut back in
                      autumn.
Illustration: *Viola tricolor* (Heartsease,
                      Wild Pansy).

Violet

Viola   Violaceae

Violets are the smallest members of the Viola
family which includes pansies and the flowers
commonly called violas. Very hardy, dwarf plants
with profuse and often sweetly scented flowers in
white, pale mauve and the colour by which they
are known; violet. Occasionally flowers shade
between white and violet. The flowers nestle
amidst mounds of dark green, heart-shaped
leaves. Very good for naturalizing amongst grass
and for underplanting trees and shrubs, as well as
in rock gardens and containers. Violets are often
to be found in sheltered hedgerows and wild
woods.

Flowering Period: Late spring to summer.
Cultivation: In moist but well-drained
fertile soil in cool semi-shade,
or in full sun where it is not
too hot.
Propagation: By seed in autumn or division
in spring.
Gardening tip: Is invasive and needs to be
trimmed back frequently unless
grown in a wild situation.
Illustration: *Viola odorata* (Sweet Violet).

Wallflower

Cheiranthus   Cruciferae

Fully to half hardy perennials and sub-shrubs,
some of which are evergreen or semi-evergreen.
Perennials are usually grown as biennials. Popular
for bedding and borders, smaller species for rock
gardens. Fragrant four-petalled flowers are
clustered on branching stems with lance-shaped
mid- to dark-green leaves. Flower colours include
white, yellow, orange, red, bronze and purple, as
well as a range of pale colours.

Flowering Period: Spring to early summer.
Cultivation: In any fertile soil in an open
                       sunny site.
Propagation: By seed in spring or by
                       softwood cuttings in summer.
Gardening tip: Plant in the vicinity of a
                       garden seat to enjoy the
                       fragrance of the flowers.
Illustration: *Cheiranthus cheiri* (common or
                       English Wallflower).

Waterlily

Nymphaea   Nymphaeaceae

Deciduous, perennial, rhizomatous water plant with floating leaves; fully hardy to frost-tender. Serenely beautiful cup or star-shaped flowers float or are carried just above the surface of the water, surrounded by floating, rounded leaves often streaked or mottled in bronze or purple. Single or semi-double flowers are often pure white with prominent golden stamens; others are blue, yellow, pink or red. Some species are night-flowering. They are a luxuriant presence in any water garden.

Flowering Period:	Summer.
Cultivation:	Require still water, preferably in an open, sunny site. Large plants may need a three foot depth of water but small-leaved plants can be grown in as little as three inches.
Propagation:	By seed or by separating plantlets in spring or early summer.
Gardening tip:	Floating leaves help reduce the spread of algae, besides providing shelter for fish.
Illustration:	*Nymphaea marliacea* "Albida".

Wind flower
(Wood anemone)

Anemone   Ranunculaceae

Fully to frost-hardy tuberous or rhizomatous
plants, smaller relatives of anemones described
earlier. Delicate stems bear solitary white or pale
mauve, sometimes fragrant flowers with
prominent yellow stamens. Very good for
naturalizing in a woodland garden, where their
vigorous growth carpets the earth with a mass of
starry flowers amidst a profusion of mid-green,
deeply divided leaves.

Flowering Period:	Spring and early summer.
Cultivation:	In moist but well-drained soil rich in humus, in full light or semi-shade.
Propagation:	By seed in late summer, by division in spring, or by root cuttings in winter.
Gardening tip:	Can be invasive. Plant in an area where it will not swamp less vigorous plants.
Illustration:	*Anemone sylvestris* (Snowdrop windflower).

Woodruff

Galium also *Asperula*   Rubiaceae

Clump-forming, fully to frost-hardy annuals and perennials. A mound of loose stems bearing leaves which can be glossy or hairy, green or grey, and masses of small, pale pink or white flowers.

Flowering Period:	Early to mid-summer.
Cultivation:	Most species thrive in very well-drained soil in full sun although some prefer shade, but all like moisture at the roots.
Propagation:	By seed or softwood cuttings in early summer, or by division in early spring or autumn.
Gardening tip:	Dislikes winter wet on crown. Protect by cloche.
Illustration:	*Galium odoratum* syn. *Asperula odorata*.

Wood sorrel

Oxalis   Oxalidaceae

Tuberous, rhizomatous or fibrous rooted
perennials and semi-evergreen sub-shrubs, fully
hardy to frost-tender. Plants form mats or tufts
of characteristic clover-like leaves with three or
more leaflets. Delicate stems bear five-petalled
flowers which in bud are rolled like umbrellas.
Colours include pink, red and purple. Flowers
and frequently leaves close up at night. Good for
rock gardens and woodland planting.

Flowering Period:	Mainly late spring or summer; *O. lobata* in autumn.
Cultivation:	In well-drained but moist soil in sun or partial shade.
Propagation:	By division in early spring or summer.
Gardening tip:	Lift tender plants in winter or provide protection with cloches.
Illustration:	*Oxalis deppei.*

Yarrow

Achillea   **Compositae**

Fully hardy perennials, many of which are
evergreen. Mainly upright plants with feathery
foliage and large, usually plate-like flower heads.
Leaves are often silvery; many are aromatic when
crushed. Flowers are long lasting, mainly yellow
but some white or pink; may be dried for winter
decoration. Tall species are suitable for borders,
smaller ones for rock gardens.

Flowering Period: Summer.
Cultivation: In any well-drained soil in the
                       sun.
Propagation: By division in early spring or
                       summer, or by softwood
                       cuttings in early summer.
Gardening tip: Tall species need staking.
Illustration: *Achillea filipendulina* "Gold
                       plate".

Zephyr lily

(Flower of the west wind, rain lily)

Zephyrantes   Amaryllidaceae

Fully to frost-hardy clump-forming bulbs with
starry, crocus-like flowers borne singly on leafless
stems. Basal leaves are narrow and semi-erect.
Flowers are white, sometimes tinged with pink,
yellow or rose-red. Suitable for naturalizing in
grass and underplanting trees and shrubs, and for
containers.

Flowering Period:	Generally late summer to autumn but some species in spring.
Cultivation:	In moist but well-drained soil in a sheltered, sunny site.
Propagation:	By seed in spring or autumn.
Gardening tip:	Mulch in winter where hardy, otherwise lift and store in frost-free conditions over winter.
Illustration:	*Zephyrantes candida* (Zephyr lily).

Zinnia

Zinnia   **Compositae**

Half hardy annuals popular as bedding and border plants; excellent for cutting. Sturdy plants with oval to lance-shaped leaves and bold, dahlia-like flowers, single, fully and semi-double, in a wide colour range including white, cream, yellow, orange, pink, red and purple as well as bicolours.

Flowering Period: Late summer to autumn.
Cultivation: In well-drained but moist and fertile soil in full sun.
Propagation: By seed in early spring.
Gardening tip: Dead-head regularly.
Illustration: *Zinnia elegans.*

Glossary of Terms

Annual: Plant growing from seed to flowering in one year then dying.

Axil: The angle between a leaf and stem, where an axillary bud develops.

Bedding plant: One that is planted to make a temporary display.

Bicoloured: Having two colours on the same petals.

Biennial: Plant grown from seed in one year, flowering the next, then dying.

Bract: A modified leaf at the base of a flower, often large and brightly coloured.

Bulb: Swollen underground bud by which some plants persist while dormant.

Bulbil: Small, immature bulb, generally at base of parent bulb but sometimes in a leaf axil.

Calyx: (plural **calyces**) The outer part of a flower that encloses the petals in bud and is formed from the *sepals*.

Climber: A plant that requires support and climbs over trellises and other structures, although some climbers are self-clinging.

Corm: Swollen underground stem base for food storage.

Corolla: The inner part of a flower, formed from the *petals*.

Cultivar: Variety of plant that has been selected and reproduced vegetatively.

Cutting: Section of a plant that is removed and used for propagation. Various types of cuttings are: **Basal**, taken from the base of the plant: **Softwood** or **greenwood**, taken from the tip of young growth;

	Semi-ripe, half-ripened wood taken during the growing season; **Ripe**, mature wood taken at the end of the growing season.
Dead-head:	To remove spent flower heads.
Deciduous:	Losing its leaves annually at the end of the growing season.
Division:	A method of propagation by which a clump is divided into several parts during dormancy.
Evergreen:	Retaining its leaves through the winter, older leaves being shed regularly throughout the year.
Floret:	A single flower in a head of many flowers.
Glaucous:	Bluish-white, bluish-green or bluish-grey.
Herbaceous:	Dying down at the end of the growing season.
Hybrid:	Plant resulting from crossing two botanically distinct plants (often denoted by the sign x).
Layering:	Method of propagation: stem is induced to root by being pegged down in the soil while it is still attached to the parent plant.
Leaflet:	The subdivision of a compound leaf.
Mulch:	Soil covering of leaf mould, peat or other substance for the purpose of improving the soil and conserving moisture.
Offset:	A small plant that arises by natural reproduction, usually at the base of the mother plant.
Panicle:	A branched *raceme*
Perennial:	Plant that grows for a number of years, generally flowering each year.
Pistil:	The female part of a flower, comprising the *ovary*, *stigma* and *style*.

Raceme: A number of short-stalked flowers borne singly along one stem, the youngest at the apex.

Rhizome: An underground, creeping stem that acts as a storage organ and bears leafy shoots.

Self-seed: To produce seedlings round the parent plant.

Sepal: Segment of a *calyx*, usually green but sometimes coloured and showy.

Shrub: A plant with woody stems branching near or from the base.

Sub-shrub: A plant that is woody at the base but with terminal shoots that die back in winter.

Spadix: (plural **spadices**) A spike-like flower cluster that is usually fleshy (characteristic of Arum).

Spathe: A large *bract*, or sometimes two, surrounding a spadix or individual flower bud.

Spike: A column of unstalked flowers.

Stamen: The male part of a flower, comprising the pollen producing *anther* and the *filament* on which it is usually borne.

Succulent: Plant with fleshy, moisture conserving leaves and/or stems.

Tendril: Thread-like structure used by some climbing plants to anchor themselves to supports.

Tuber: Swollen underground organ, deriving from stem or root, for food storage.

Woody: With a stem composed of woody fibres and vessels; in contrast to soft-stemmed or *herbaceous*.

Index